THE WORLDS OF ARCHITECTURAL DIGEST

CHATEAUX AND VILLAS

THE WORLDS OF ARCHITECTURAL DIGEST

CHATEAUX AND VILLAS

EDITED BY PAIGE RENSE

EDITOR-IN-CHIEF, ARCHITECTURAL DIGEST

THE KNAPP PRESS   PUBLISHERS   LOS ANGELES

Published in the United States of America in 1982
The Knapp Press
5900 Wilshire Boulevard, Los Angeles, California 90036
Copyright© 1982 by Knapp Communications Corporation
All rights reserved
First Edition

Distributed by The Viking Press
625 Madison Avenue, New York, New York 10022

Distributed simultaneously in Canada by Penguin Books Canada Limited

Library of Congress Cataloging in Publication Data
Main entry under title: Chateaux and villas.
(The Worlds of Architectural digest)
Selections from the pages of Architectural digest,
newly edited and designed.
1. Interior decoration. 2. Interior architecture.
I. Rense, Paige. II. Architectural digest.
NK2130.C48   1982   747′.8882   82-8968
AACR2

ISBN 0-89535-101-3
Printed and bound in the United States of America

CONTENTS

FOREWORD

Surprising as it may sometimes seem in our modern, ever-changing world, there are still corners of the earth that remain today much as they were in centuries past. Visit the hills of Tuscany, and you find landscapes that are depicted in Renaissance paintings. Wander through the gardens and rural villages of Japan, and you are transported to a world portrayed by Hiroshige more than a hundred years ago.

So it is with the stately châteaux and villas featured in this volume. Seeing them today in all their splendor and glory somehow brings the past immediately alive. Perhaps it is because they were originally built as homes; no matter how grand or monumental they may be, they were conceived and created in human terms.

What I find especially appealing about the many châteaux and villas in the pages of ARCHITECTURAL DIGEST is that most of them continue to be lived in today—in some cases by descendants of the families for whom they were built centuries ago. Some present-day owners cherish and preserve all vestiges of the historic past. The Rothschild family, for example, works with the National Trust of Great Britain to maintain the priceless collections of European antiques housed in *Waddesdon Manor,* a Buckinghamshire estate built by Baron Ferdinand de Rothschild of Vienna in the late nineteenth century. Prince Bonifazio Meli Lupi lives amid the late-Renaissance and Gothic treasures his family has assembled since the seventeenth century in their thousand-year-old ducal castle, *La Rocca di Soragna.*

In other cases, the owners have managed to maintain a respect for cultural heritage while creating interiors that are wholly personal and often contemporary in style. The noted international collector Evelyn Kelly Lambert has assembled a collection of twentieth-century art that seems entirely at ease with the Renaissance wall panels and ceiling frescoes of her villa near Vicenza, Italy. At the *Château de Detilly*, in the valley of the Loire, Parisian antiques dealer and interior designer Alain Demachy has tried, in his own words, "to avoid any slavish imitation of the past"; his seventeenth-century home is decorated in a thoroughly modern manner, with a discriminating blend of antique and contemporary appointments.

As the examples may suggest, the twenty châteaux and villas in this volume share a fundamental characteristic of all great interior design: while each may represent a specific period and style, it remains strikingly unique, stamped with the individuality of its owners. A legacy of the past, each one remains vibrantly alive today.

Paige Rense
Editor-in-Chief
Los Angeles, California

THE WORLDS OF ARCHITECTURAL DIGEST

CHATEAUX AND VILLAS

WADDESDON MANOR

Members of the Rothschild family, over a period of more than a century, have assembled at *Waddesdon Manor* one of the world's great art collections in a rare and sumptuous house. Everything in this grand estate set in the Buckinghamshire countryside imparts the thrill of matchless quality—a standard that extends to an astounding range of the arts, all the way from French furniture and Gainsborough portraits to painted fans and decorative buttons.

Quite apart from the treasures it contains, Waddesdon is a home made distinctive by the family who built and still maintains it. Four different Rothschilds created this collection. The first of the four strands in the plait was formed by Baron Ferdinand, of Vienna. Between 1874 and 1899, he built Waddesdon as his ideal house, using the French architect Destailleur to incorporate the architectural details he admired in the great châteaux. He filled his house with the cream of the ancien régime mise-en-scène he so loved, creating the culturally extravagant but livable family house and exquisitely landscaped grounds that remain today. When Baron Ferdinand died in 1898, he left the estate to his sister, Alice de Rothschild, known to everyone as "Miss Alice."

The second of the strands was formed by Miss Alice. Her self-imposed task was to conserve and maintain the home. Famous for her tough discipline, she was a superbly able and creative collector in her own right. She replaced the Renaissance contents of the smoking room and the adjoining passage (their former contents having been donated by Baron Ferdinand to the British Museum as the Waddesdon Bequest) with an intriguing array of rare arms and armor, Limoges enamels, majolica, Continental glass, miniatures and Italian paintings.

The next strand was started in 1922, when Waddesdon was bequeathed by Miss Alice to her great-nephew, the husband of Mrs. James de Rothschild. The couple found the surprise inheritance immediately "lovely and habitable." James de Rothschild's varied interests and lucid personality, together with his eventual great inheritance of other furniture and objects of art from his parents—the legendary Paris collectors Baron and Baroness Edmond de Rothschild—crowned the happiness at Waddesdon.

Thus, Baron Ferdinand, Miss Alice and James de Rothschild laid out three strands of Waddesdon's gilded plait. These have been lastingly interwoven with a fourth strand, that of Mrs. James de Rothschild, who, since her husband's death in 1957, has worked with the National Trust to maintain the family collection. The oldest living member of the Rothschild family, Mrs. de Rothschild has often had reason to recall the words of her friend Lord d'Abernon upon hearing that she and her husband had inherited the manor: "Waddesdon is not an inheritance; it is a career." There is not a trace of sensationalism as she reflects and talks with complete authority about Waddesdon's past, present and future. Conversation ranges easily from memories about Miss Alice or a royal visit, to the technicalities of lighting, to wall fabrics and adaptations of décor and layout. This penetrating attention to detail has been part of Waddesdon's story from the beginning.

In 1897, the creator of Waddesdon hoped: "May the day yet be distant when the weeds will spread over the gardens, the terraces crumble into dust, the pictures and cabinets cross the Channel or the Atlantic, and the melancholy cry of the night-jar sound from the deserted towers." James de Rothschild, by his priceless gift to the British people, and Mrs. James de Rothschild, by her dedication in maintaining standards that are unique in the world, have calmly advanced that date into eternity.

PRECEDING PAGE: *The creator of Waddesdon Manor and of its unparalleled art collection was Baron Ferdinand de Rothschild, the first of three generations of Rothschilds who contributed to the resplendence of this French château in the English countryside.* ABOVE: *Giuliano Mozani's Fountain of Triton and Nereids heralds the approach to the house.* RIGHT: *Exotic birds are kept in the wrought-iron aviary.*

ABOVE: *The intimacy of the 18th-century French statue* Venus Arming Cupid *contrasts with the heroic architecture.* LEFT: *The central grotto of the Aviary reveals its intricate design. Identical wings, on either side of the grotto, are divided into flight cages. Behind each of these a heated inner compartment shelters the birds in cold weather. A kitchen, a hospital and breeding cages complete the aviary facilities.*

The Morning Room glows with silk damask and royal
Savonnerie rugs generally acknowledged to be among the
finest in existence. Above the marble fireplace is Sir Joshua
Reynolds's portrait of Emily Pott as Thaïs. Chairs covered
in Beauvais tapestry surround a Louis XV mechanical
table. The two small portraits are by Gainsborough.

Gainsborough's portrait of Master Nicholls, The Pink Boy, *graces another Morning Room wall. The writing table, at right, was made in 1786 under the direction of Beneman and Kemp for Louis XVI. Some of Baron Ferdinand's rare 18th-century volumes fill the bookcase. On its top is a pair of ewers with French ormolu mounts.*

TOP: *Mirror frames made for the Hôtel de Villars in Paris embellish the Dining Room. The large Beauvais tapestry was designed by Boucher. The dining table displays 18th-century porcelain figures.* ABOVE: *The East Gallery is distinguished by two panoramic views of Venice by Francesco Guardi.*

TOP: *Artworks in The Baron's Room include portraits by Reynolds, on the left, and George Romney. A Fragonard drawing rests on an easel.* ABOVE: *Mirrors in the Green Boudoir reflect paneling from the duc de Richelieu's house in Paris.* OPPOSITE: *The Portico Bedroom is festooned with floral fabric.*

LE CLOS FIORENTINA

One of the oldest houses on the eastern Côte d'Azur, *Le Clos Fiorentina* was built into the rocks above the Mediterranean in the early nineteenth century. In 1975 it was bought by the present owners, who, with the help of interior designer David Hicks, transformed it into a home of witty contrasts—raffia-covered floors under a Louis XV marquetry secretary, *bois doré* Regency consoles surmounted by a Sam Francis painting, fine Louis XVI chairs wrapped in crisp cotton prints designed by Mr. Hicks. The house also means life out-of-doors —by the surf, beside the pool or in the garden. Luncheon is served at the pool house, dinner on the terrace. The terrace looks toward the Alpes Maritimes, but the views from the house are of the sea.

Mr. Hicks borrowed colors from the surrounding landscape. Shunning commonplace "swimming-pool turquoise," he lined the pool with terrazzo tiling in deep Mediterranean blue. "It's the exact color of the sea below," he says. Salt water is pumped from the sea up to the pool. Days are spent beside it, and often balmy evenings as well. "The pool pavilion was a Germanic 1930 structure—very cold and forbidding," Mr. Hicks recalls. He clothed it in Etruscan-red sailcloth, similar to the Côte's craggy cliffs.

The main house is the marriage of the owner's fondness for antiques and Mr. Hicks's style of simplified elegance. With his Paris associates Christian Badin and Barbara Werth, the designer attempted to take advantage of the spectacular location while also preserving the original personality of the villa. "I was helped by the fact that I'd known the home for years and had stayed there many times," he says. "The new owners didn't want it to look too new or too decorated." The wall separating the living and dining rooms was torn down, making one large space. "Now the main living room has a dining table

in it, in the French tradition," Mr. Hicks says. "After all, the French never really had dining rooms until the 1840s. The living room was very dark and had no windows on one side. To add them we had to dynamite part of the mountain." The house was completely replumbed and air-conditioned, and a modern professional kitchen capable of serving forty people was installed. The work took one year, partly because of the difficulty in obtaining permits, partly out of concern for the gardens. During the pool construction a special bridge was built so that trucks could enter without damaging the plants.

It was the gardens, designed by the previous resident, that first attracted the present owners to the house. "They are built on a series of terraces in the hillside," Mr. Hicks explains, "and they are made up of smaller individual gardens." There is a walkway edged with white camellias, the shrubs protected from the glare of the Mediterranean sun by rattan roofs, which are a common sight in the south of France. The colors of the gardens are limited primarily to blue, gray, white and green. In a nice Alice in Wonderland touch, the trunks of the trees have been painted white, adding to the color scheme.

The design for the present interiors created by Mr. Hicks was total, even to the details of accoutrements for entertaining. He arranged for porcelain dinner service, silver flatware, linens and accessories. The owners spend only summers at Le Clos Fiorentina, although some decades ago the Côte d'Azur was primarily a fashionable winter resort. When they are in residence, they entertain often. With this in mind, Mr. Hicks, who has a house in the neighborhood, has created an uncluttered space for informal living. "It's modern life in a Directoire house with antiques and good pictures," he says, "in one of the most beautiful settings in the world."

PRECEDING PAGE: *Le Clos Fiorentina was built more than a century before cliff locations became fashionable for villas on the Côte d'Azur. British designer David Hicks was intent on "preserving the exquisite gardens."*

BELOW AND OPPOSITE: *The former Living Room and Dining Room were combined to make one large area, in which Louis XVI chairs covered in fresh fabrics create a country atmosphere. A painting by Roy Lichtenstein dominates the far wall. The antique chimneypiece is of limestone; on it is a Benin bronze relief, and nearby is a painting of a cat by Andy Warhol.*

BELOW LEFT: *Beside the bed in a Master Bedroom is a Regency mahogany table.* LOWER LEFT: *A Bath is appointed with 18th-century engravings.* BELOW RIGHT: *Another Master Bedroom features a Louis XV desk. A mask by Robert Courtright rests atop the commode.* OPPOSITE: *The Dining Terrace overlooks the Alpes Maritimes.*

14

THE DUKE OF WELLINGTON'S COUNTRY ESTATE

After the great victory of Waterloo, the duke of Wellington was hailed as the savior of his country. Parliament voted to spend £600,000 to acquire an appropriate house and estate for the nation's hero. The Great Duke, after turning down thirteen other properties, chose *Stratfield Saye House*, not far from Reading. A visit to the house is a journey into the victorious past, for the atmosphere of the nineteenth century and the Great Duke's time is still very much present there. Even the voice of the famous warrior seems to linger; just inside the main entrance there is a notice board, put up by the first duke, that reads: "Those desirous of seeing the Interior of the House are requested to ring at the door of entrance and to express their desire. It is wished that the practice of stopping on the paved walk to look in at the windows should be discontinued."

The eighth and present duke of Wellington inherited the estate in 1972. The Great Duke found Stratfield Saye a drain on his financial resources, and the present duke describes the challenge: "As someone who owns a great historical house in the ducal context, I regard myself as owner, but I also feel myself to be simply custodian for my life. I look forward to the house being enjoyed and being carried on for at least another two generations. Stratfield Saye has a special feeling for me, a feeling of continuum with the family. Sometimes, sitting alone in the dining room in the evening, I long for the walls to speak and tell me the story of what has gone on in this room. What scenes the walls have witnessed! Wellington's friends, kings and queens around the table. I long to know everything there is to know about it all."

Stratfield Saye lies on the old Roman road from London to Bath. The house is in the center of a park, approached by several drives, and below the six-acre main lawn on the east front flows the river Loddon.

The present residence was built about 1630, and in the eighteenth century Lord Rivers spent fifteen years improving the house and landscaping the park. The Jacobean gardens and formal rides were dispensed with and, in the manner of Capability Brown and Humphry Repton, the surroundings were transformed and opened up. Groves of cedars of Lebanon, pines and tulip trees were planted, and the streams of the Loddon were merged into a broad river. Renovations included pulling down the old church, which was thought to be too near the house and too ugly, and the rebuilding of a new Palladian church at the end of one of the graceful avenues radiating from the manor. The Great Duke added the conservatory and two outer wings in the mid-nineteenth century. He also introduced central heating and the intriguing water closets with double doors that are found in many of the bedrooms.

It is not possible to describe the multitude of pictures, carpets, furniture and treasures in the many rooms of the house. In the cellars and attics, too, there are trunks meticulously packed with belongings from the days of the Great Duke. Documents are still, even now, coming to light. Tributes, memorabilia and remembrances of battles long won, images of Wellington and the fruits of victory, are everywhere. In a place where such a sense of history lives on, where there is so much to record, restore and conserve, what is the single most important quality in ownership? The eighth duke of Wellington replies: "Pride in being responsible, the pride of possession, the pride of looking after Stratfield Saye. I *love* the house. I ought to do everything possible to safeguard it for the future. Sometimes the burdens are heavy—taxes, servants—and one wants to take the line of least resistance. But every sacrifice is worth it to preserve such historic houses."

Two years after his victory at the Battle of Waterloo, in
1815, the duke of Wellington was given Stratfield Saye
House by a grateful nation. PRECEDING PAGE: The oval
Courtyard of Honor, purposefully devoid of fountains and
flowers, is the center from which allées extend. ABOVE: In
the Gallery, a background of gold surrounds engravings
of scenes from Shakespeare. Adding to the splendor are
Louis XVI cabinets, in the style of Boulle, and ornate pedes-
tals. The bronze busts are of French and English nobility.
RIGHT: Souvenirs and trophies in the Main Hall recall the
triumphs of the Great Duke. The paintings beneath the
balcony depict scenes of the war on the Iberian Peninsula.
The malachite tazza on a table in front of the fireplace
was a gift from the duke's ally, Czar Alexander I.

18

OPPOSITE: *The ceiling of the Drawing Room duplicates the Rococo ornamentation of Chippendale mirrors. French and Dutch paintings belonged to Joseph Bonaparte.* LEFT: *Double doors lead from the Drawing Room to a small Cardroom. The Dutch paintings include scenes by van Goyen and Teniers.*

LEFT: *An Empire console supported by two gilded sphinxes, in the Dining Room, was bought by the first duke at the 1816 sale of the possessions of Cardinal Fesch. It is flanked by gilt-gesso torchières. The portraits on the wall above are by Sir Thomas Lawrence.*

Pale silk wallcovering lightens the effect of elaborate detailing and a coffered ceiling in the Library. Tub chairs and Regency writing tables rest on a Feraghan rug. Over the mantelpiece is The Ascension *by Tintoretto.*

A button-tufted silk brocade bed in the Salamanca Suite is
flanked by a pair of Victorian fruitwood side tables displaying Etruscan-style lamps with overlay shades. The
wall is covered in silk damask. The paintings are Italian.

ART AT THE VILLA LAMBERT

"I prefer to acquire the work of an artist before meeting the artist personally," says Mrs. Evelyn Kelly Lambert as she moves through the most impressive cross section of contemporary art ever to grace a villa in the countryside around Venice. "Knowing them happens later, of course, but when it comes to deciding, I don't want to be influenced by the artist's personality." This is just the sort of perceptive remark you would expect to hear from this extraordinary lady from Tennessee, whose active life, travels and personality have charmed the art circles in many countries on several continents.

It has always been thus—since the 1930s in Havana, where Mrs. Lambert studied, married a Cuban and was soon immersed in the culture of Spain. Long trips to Europe meant the protean art scene of Paris, where incense smoldered before the work of Picasso and Dali. Widowhood and the war took her to California. There her days were filled with war work, committee posts and earning a living. But somehow she found time to haunt the galleries, and gradually her collection grew. By the time she met and married Texan Joseph Olliphant Lambert, a year or so after the war, Mrs. Lambert owned an extensive collection of then-contemporary paintings that she shipped to Dallas to display in their large and accommodating penthouse. Olliphant Lambert was a distinguished landscape architect who, as his widow stoutly claims, "had more to do with making Dallas beautiful than anybody in the Southwest." Her own efforts were no less energetic and effective. As a member of the board of directors of the Dallas Museum of Contemporary Arts, she plunged into such avant-garde activities as arranging the first Claes Oldenburg happenings.

"When my husband retired, in the 1960s," says Mrs. Lambert, "he decided to live in Europe, as far away from business as he could get." As it turned out, he "retired" to an even more difficult job. It seems that the Marchese Roi, instrumental in the reconstruction and preservation of Palladian villas in the Venice hinterland, had suggested to the Lamberts that they purchase one of these magnificent but dilapidated country seats for themselves. The Lamberts were fired by the idea. Even so, it was two years before they entered the abandoned park of the villa in a hamlet outside Vicenza. For two seasons Mr. Lambert worked on the gardens while Mrs. Lambert, with architect Francesco Gnecchi Ruscone, tackled the house. By June 1970, they were able to move in, but it proved to be a tragic beginning. Having put his garden in order, Mr. Lambert died. The park remains his last fine work.

For another three years Mrs. Lambert kept the penthouse in Dallas. When she did decide to transfer her art collection to Italy, she called the designer with whom she had worked for thirty years, Robert Wedel; his specialty was the installation of paintings in residences. Mr. Wedel assisted in the Herculean task of shipping the collection from Dallas and installing and arranging what were to be the nucleus of the Villa Lambert display: pieces by Dali, Lucio Fontana, Jean Arp and Calder—to name a few.

Mrs. Lambert, her height accentuated by her famous upswept hairdo (immortalized by Cecil Beaton in a witty sketch) belongs with those fabulous international figures who have added sparkle to Venice down the ages. Like most personalities larger than life, she loves new faces as much as old friends. The footsteps of friends and strangers sound in the halls of Villa Lambert, and guest rooms are seldom empty while Mrs. Lambert is in residence. Dinners, concerts and performances by the lake are as much a part of the lively scene as are her works of art.

24

The centuries converge in the Villa Lambert near Vicenza, where American art patron Evelyn Kelly Lambert has assembled her collection of contemporary paintings and sculpture. PRECEDING PAGE: *In the 18th century, a Neo-Classical facade and two long wings were added to the original residence, a 16th-century farmhouse.* BELOW AND OPPOSITE: *The generous scale of the Salon encourages inventive groupings of art and objects. A processional fiberglass sculpture by Oginio Balderi provides a welcome at the entrance; overhead is Timothy Hennessy's painted banner.*

OPPOSITE: *In the Salon, color and form direct the visual flow from corner paintings by Castellani to Nexo's wall sculpture, Youngerman's* Tondo Black on White, *Celentano's achromatic* December 30 *and Fontana's* Spatial Concept. OPPOSITE BELOW: *In the Study artworks include, left of the doorway, Polesello's fusing circles, Dorazio's bright rectangles and a small Baumeister study; above the door, Calder's* Starfish Trail; *right, Olitski's irregular circles; Rietveld's* Red-Blue Chair *and, on a low table, Dali's* Lady Giraffe. BELOW: *The 16th-century frescoes in the Garden Room are attributed to Veronese and his followers.*

OPPOSITE: *In the Small Dining Room, walls are covered with 16th-century panels, probably the work of Ludovico Pozzoserrato. The realistic likeness of a youth, which may have been painted by Veronese, calls to mind the villa's Renaissance inhabitants.* BELOW: *A primitive portrait of Mrs. Lambert's mother surveys the Master Bedroom—an oasis of exuberant color and small playful objects. The delicate ceiling frescoes were painted in the 18th century.*

31

NORMANDY RETREAT

"The marvelous thing about Deauville is that it's near Paris and far from the ocean," said Sem, the caricaturist and chronicler of *Tout Paris* at the turn of the century, employing the bored and sophisticated irony of his day. For Deauville most certainly is on the ocean, but it is—like neighboring Trouville—a beach resort only in the sense that Vichy and Baden-Baden are nothing more than spas. At the turn of the century wealthy Parisians went to Deauville as they went to Nice and Cannes, to see their friends and to frequent the grand hotels and casinos and racetracks. But today there is far more to this part of Normandy than the glittering social scene. Not far away, for example, past the forest of Chantepie, is the tiny village of Saint-André-d'Hébertot, where a church and a rectory and a cluster of houses are huddled together at the edge of a park. Through the branches of trees that are hundreds of years old can be seen the *Château de Saint-André-d'Hébertot,* now the home of the marquis and marquise d'Aulan.

The original plan for the château conceived by the seigneur de Trouville in 1630 allowed for four wings to be joined by corridors to form a vast courtyard. The main façade was to open onto a large and formal French garden. Happily, funds soon ran out, for such a grandiose project would have been out of place in this corner of Normandy. In any event, the seigneur built only one of the proposed corner wings as a point of departure for the main façade. Many years later, during the Second Empire, when the duc de Morny—the half-brother of Napoleon III —founded Deauville and created its elegant amusements, a wealthy banker came into possession of the château. To impress the haut monde who frequented nearby Deauville, he built a tower and added another wing to the structure. In matters of decoration he gave free rein to Second Empire taste.

"I knew right away that I had to change everything," says the marquise d'Aulan, recalling her first visit to the château with her husband. To preside over the family business, they were obliged to live in a townhouse in Reims, one of the provincial capitals of Champagne. But they decided to find a quiet oasis for themselves. The marquis had happy memories of Deauville since he enjoyed playing polo and delighted in the sporting atmosphere of the resort. And he had fallen in love with the quiet countryside where the Château de Saint-André-d'Hébertot was located. When they purchased the property, the marquise set about turning the ornate château into a pleasant country house. With the help of her friend Suzanne Magliano, she did exactly that.

"The sunlight and the outdoors flood every part of the house," says the marquise. "It is almost like a greenhouse, and there are little glassed-in terraces where you can sit and appreciate the countryside. It's a transparent house, and I wanted to make it even more so. But, above everything else, I wanted to recapture the simple and elegant spirit of the eighteenth century." Today, the château is welcoming and agreeable through every season of the year. The décor is light and uncomplicated, and there is no important antique furniture, just unassuming Normandy chairs and comfortable sofas. The unity of the interior design is found in the delightful interplay of colors—primarily of blue and white.

With such a comfortable retreat, the owners rarely go to Deauville. They much prefer the country life. The marquis and marquise d'Aulan are content to occupy themselves with their children and their guests. They are happy to spend holidays in their small paradise, where horses run free and cows graze in the pastures. Their world is private, far from both the highways and the summer beaches.

Great sweeps of lawn and a trout-filled moat set off the classic symmetry of the Marquis and Marquise François d'Aulan's Normandy country home, Château de Saint-André-d'Hébertot. PRECEDING PAGE AND LEFT: *Corner towers, one dating from the 17th century and one from the 19th, flank the main body of the residence—an 18th-century structure that measures only 16 feet in width.* BELOW: *Assisted by her friend Suzanne Magliano, the marquise restored the château's unpretentious elegance and created a winter-garden effect in the Entrance Hall.*

35

BELOW: *Elaborately carved Louis XIV boiserie, stripped to its natural oaken beauty, envelops the Salon in warmth. The 18th-century marble fireplace serves as the focal point for a seating arrangement composed of commodious armchairs and a sofa upholstered in a light Sardinian linen.*
OPPOSITE: *Checked and floral fabrics lend a harmony of hue to the Dining Room. Here the paneling is painted a muted shade, with light accents, to emphasize the color of the tapestrylike painted canvas between the windows.*

HOMAGE TO BRITTANY'S PAST

"Nine times out of ten," says Serge Royaux, "when people contact a particular interior designer, they are already well acquainted with his or her work." So he was more than a little surprised when an unknown voice asked him over the telephone to undertake the construction and complete design of a house in Brittany. With some trepidation, M. Royaux traveled west from Paris to assess the situation, but his fears were dispelled when he met the comte and comtesse de Tugny in a small Gothic manor house in the country, where they were then living. The designer felt completely at home. Indeed, their house—with its low ceilings and chestnut beams, its slate floors and rough plaster walls—reminded Serge Royaux of the thrust of his own work.

Unhappily, career considerations required the owners to move from this gracious country home to the neighboring city of Pontivy. At first they had hoped to find some old house there with all the characteristics of French provincial architecture, a house they could renovate completely. However, nothing they found appealed to them, and they decided to build something along the lines of the country seat they were leaving. Their requirements were not overly demanding: a garage large enough to contain a collection of antique automobiles; a garden that would suggest the country, and nothing of the city; and an interior arrangement that would allow them to live simply, with a minimum of staff. In addition, the house would have to conform to the urban landscape of Pontivy itself. The town is an interesting one. Created by the emperor Napoleon as the capital of the province of Brittany, for the first thirty years of its existence it bore the name Napoléonville. Its founding was an echo of what Peter the Great had done at St. Petersburg. From Le Palais de la Préfecture to the square surrounded by adminis-

trative buildings, Pontivy is still, even today, the very prototype of governmental Neo-Classicism.

Serge Royaux, who has always transformed his favorite Classical styles into the more simplified idiom of contemporary design, was much intrigued with Pontivy's architectural purity and the liberal use of unyielding granite. To keep the de Tugny residence in harmony with the row of private houses along the quai where it stands—barracks across the canal are similar in appearance—he joined the basic shells of two existing buildings to create a common façade. The resulting house has a stone cornice, small-paned windows, a mansard roof and a balcony in the seventeenth-century manner. "In fifteen years this house will look like an antique," says the designer. Extensive antique boiseries and an enormous stone fireplace determine the height of the ceilings, the size of the rooms and the general interior arrangement. The varnished chestnut ceilings recall the open beams of the count and countess's former house in the country, while the plantings in the garden, and the trees that line the banks of the canal outside, echo the rural scene.

One particular passion of M. Royaux is evident everywhere—his delight in contrasting natural materials. The use of marble and granite and thick wood as backgrounds has allowed him to mix the furniture and objects from different periods and to point up their underlying affinities. The owners followed Serge Royaux's work with enthusiasm, and, as well as a mutuality of taste, they shared with him a love of collecting. Indeed, their tastes are catholic: ancient weaponry, antique automobiles, turn-of-the-century sandstone, old kitchen utensils. And perhaps it is this richness of incident that gives such a vital character to what may well be one of the last private houses to be built in "Napoléonville."

Designer Serge Royaux deftly blended modern under-statement and traditional grace for the Brittany home of the comte and comtesse de Tugny. PRECEDING PAGE: *The newly constructed residence joins two older houses. With its slate roof, small dormer windows and wrought-iron balcony, it is well adapted to its Neo-Classical setting.* LEFT: *An 18th-century relief by Bouchardon animates the cobbled Entranceway.* BELOW: *An appealing combination of plants and highly polished woods lends warmth and vitality to the Living Room. Stately Corinthian columns emphasize the restrained formalism of the room. A large canvas by Simon Vouet bestows somber grandeur.*

A 17th-century stone fireplace offers an inviting focus for a seating arrangement composed of a sofa and chairs upholstered in wool. The petit point pillows were embroidered by Mme de Tugny. Screens of Brazilian rosewood add luster and an element of symmetry to the setting. To the right of the hearth is a lamp made from a Louis XIV vase, and at the center of the grouping stands a table displaying marble and stone bowls and obelisks.

ABOVE: *Verdant-hued pilasters and the polished wood ceiling enrich the Library, where an ornate Louis XIV cartel clock seems to hover before the mirrored fireplace surround. A handsome 18th-century* bureau à cylindre *bears a group of 19th-century Italian architectural souvenirs in marble.* OPPOSITE: *An amply draped canopy bed graces one Bedroom of the Master Suite. The stately Louis XVI desk, served by a Louis XV cane-back fauteuil, and the small 18th-century mahogany table are laden with discreet groupings of fin-de-siècle stoneware.*

Like an oversize vitrine placed on a grassy carpet, the garage displays part of the comte's collection of classic cars behind multipaned folding doors. From left to right are a 1930 Delahaye, a 1960 Mark II Jaguar, a 1937 TA MG and a 1957 XK 150 Jaguar.

CHATSWORTH IN DEVONSHIRE

When the duke of Devonshire inherited *Chatsworth*, in 1950, both he and the duchess were thirty and living in a smaller house nearby. As she speaks of that early time, when they were deciding just where to begin with structural improvements and redecoration of the great house of the Cavendish family, the duchess recalls with affection: "If we had not already known the house very well indeed, we might have done something very impulsive and very stupid—like painting the whole place pink! As it was, I was pretty slapdash in those days. But Chatsworth has a very strong feeling of its own—a sort of disciplined freedom that, we found, narrows down your options when it comes to making changes."

The history of their home began in the mid-sixteenth century, when the estate was bought by Sir William Cavendish and his wife, Elizabeth Hardwick. Their second son was made earl of Devonshire in 1618. The Elizabethan house they built exactly filled the square central part of the present structure. Toward the end of the seventeenth century, the fourth earl, who was to become the first duke, started to rework the exterior of the manor. His intention was to remodel only the south front, but building was his passion. During the next twenty-one years, therefore—until his death—the south, east and, finally, north fronts were carefully rebuilt.

Fifty years later the fourth duke, seeking an uninterrupted view from the front of the house, made vast alterations. The main entrance was relocated from the east front to the north, part of the garden was uprooted and redesigned, and the course of the river was straightened. Late in the eighteenth century, the sixth duke undertook even more extensive changes. This time the six different sections that made up the first duke's building were reconstructed to become one whole. Sir Jeffry Wyatville was commissioned to carry out the additions, among them the large north wing, which includes the theater.

Another person whose work is significant in connection with Chatsworth is the famous gardener, designer and architect Joseph Paxton, who became head gardener in the first half of the nineteenth century. His work includes the Great Conservatory, which he built for growing the exotic plants that were then being introduced to England, and the Emperor Fountain, in the Canal Pond at the south of the mansion. The Great Conservatory provided many design ideas for Paxton's Crystal Palace, which he later designed to house the Great Exhibition of 1851 in London's Hyde Park. Sadly, Chatsworth's Great Conservatory was demolished after World War I, but a new one was completed in 1970.

The full history of Chatsworth would take many pages to describe, but the impressions of its magic are immediate. At twilight there is the gleam of gold on the *outside* window frames—an idea that captured the imagination of the sixth duke when he was in Russia. Water dances down the steps from the Cascade, a terraced stream that looks like a glass stairway. Myriad colors and textures remain in the mind's eye: those golden nineteenth-century Indian curtains, the sheen of ivory silk in Sargent's portrait of three sisters, and the green of malachite.

In the drawing room, where the family gather most often, the ceiling is high and the windows tall. The view of formal grounds through them is one of majestic proportions, yet the feeling within the room itself is of comfortable informality. "Dogs and children soon ruffle up a place," says the duchess, "and Chatsworth is family life, above all. Though it's difficult to predict its future in so uncertain a world, there's no doubt that houses are built to be lived in. A house without humans is, truly, a sad place."

Chatsworth, historic seat of the Cavendish family, dukes of Devonshire, stands squarely amid its vast Derbyshire parklands. PRECEDING PAGE: *A carving of the Cavendish family arms by Samuel Watson embellishes the pediment on the west façade.* ABOVE: *In the Blue Drawing Room, Batoni portraits of Cavendish ancestors flank a Sargent portrait. The landscape is by Momper.*

In the writings of the sixth duke, the Blue Drawing Room figured as "the most joyous and frequented of all the rooms." Now it continues to be enjoyed by the eleventh duke and duchess, who have brightened the imposing background with cheerful slipcovers, books and garden flowers. Mahogany doors, installed in 1839, contrast with their carved and gilded architrave.

ABOVE: *The Leather Room takes its name from the rich gold-tooled French leather, circa 1835, that upholsters the walls and blends with an abundance of similarly tooled leather and cloth book bindings. Shelves at right contain a collection of bibles.* OPPOSITE: *In the Private Dining Room, the full-length likeness of Philip II of Spain is by Rubens, after Titian. The centerpiece is an Ascot Gold Cup won by the then-duke of Devonshire's Morion in 1891.*

Golden Indian silk brocade, purchased
in 1839, distinguishes the Yellow Drawing Room. A William and Mary églo-
misé mirror reflects Tintoretto's portrait
of a youth. Eighteenth-century English girandoles flank the Louis XVI
Sèvres biscuit clock atop the mantel.

A resplendent giltwood canopy bed,
swagged in 18th-century hand-painted
silk, dominates the Center Bedroom.
Among the paintings are works by
Guido Reni, Vanni and Wouwerman.
Graceful fluted pilasters further the
serenely noble mood of the room.

CHATEAU DE DETILLY

The valley of the Loire—with its landscapes and vineyards, its forests and fish ponds—has become a compelling symbol of the French countryside. From the many châteaux that are mirrored in the waters of the Loire and its tributaries to the village houses of white stone walls and slate roofs, there is hardly a location in the area that does not call to mind some colorful episode in French history. Thus it was at *Chinon,* within whose walls the Knights Templar were imprisoned and Joan of Arc identified her disguised king; at *Blois,* where the duc de Guise was murdered; at *Chenonceau,* palace of the lovely Diane de Poitiers, mistress of Henry II; at *Amboise,* where François I welcomed Leonardo da Vinci. No wonder this rich tapestry of history has fired the popular imagination and inspired so many writers and poets.

Every bit as romantic is that part of the Loire valley where the *Château de Detilly,* owned by Parisian antiques dealer and interior designer Alain Demachy, is located. This is Touraine, the land of Gargantua and Pantagruel, those giant rogues who leap so amiably from the pages of Rabelais. This is indeed Touraine, the land of fine wine and beautiful women, the lush and abundant garden of France.

In the traditional manner, the main rooms of the Château de Detilly are arranged on an east-west axis. M. Demachy eliminated certain nineteenth-century additions in order to create a small garden *à l'italienne.* Now double doors lead from the dining room to the terrace where meals can be taken in the summer, protected from the sun, and on mild winter days as well. Set in the midst of palm trees and bougainvillea, the château, with its tall French windows and painted front door, suggests the tropical and the colonial. "Even banana trees grow well," explains M. Demachy, "and it is only necessary to cover them with straw during the colder months."

In his career, M. Demachy has created rooms of many moods. He is well known for his contemporary interiors, which he at times softens with Far Eastern elements, and he was among the first in France to design in the Oriental style. "Here at Château de Detilly," he says, "I was interested in creating a contemporary feeling. I wanted to avoid any slavish imitation of the past." Thus, the designer treated the seventeenth-century spaces in a modern manner, with some nineteenth-century influences. By using materials characteristic of the Loire valley, terra-cotta and Angers slate, he has followed traditional formulas. In many details—armchairs designed by Emilio Terry, Second Empire sofas, lamps mounted on antique bases—Alain Demachy is more of an antiques dealer than an interior designer. In fact, he has been influential in the reinterpretation and revitalized use of antiques. "In this regard I always had a great deal of respect for my neighbor Emilio Terry. He knew exactly how to give his own *Château de Rochecotte* the atmosphere of an old family house where all sorts of styles were mixed."

M. Demachy has done something in a similar vein in his own residence. The Tower Room of the château is his tribute to the châteaux of the Loire. Here he has re-created a Neo-Gothic décor, seen in the ceiling and in the frieze surrounding the heraldic fireplace as well as in armchairs purchased from the Château de Rochecotte. Combining these elements, he has fashioned a warm room filled with family memories—on the walls are original prints by his grandfather Robert Demachy, a photographer well known at the beginning of this century. Thus, at the Château de Detilly, Alain Demachy has found the occasion to combine his two major interests: the creation of a congenial interior décor and the discovery and creative use of rare furniture and objects.

Designer Alain Demachy fashioned his château in
the Loire valley as a refined country retreat. PRECEDING
PAGE: *With its harmonious proportions and traditional
elements, the château typifies the stately architecture of
the region.* LEFT: *The blend of contemporary and antique
appointments that characterizes the décor is evident in the
Living Room. Faience jars and a Neo-Classical bronze
horse provide an antique contrast to modern artworks. The
lithographs near the mantel are by Picasso, the painting by
Léger.* ABOVE: *In the Dining Room, geometrically tiled
walls extend the pattern of stone and terra-cotta tile flooring.
Busts, classical in style, flank the 17th-century fireplace.*
FOLLOWING PAGES: *In the Living Room, woven fiber matting
on the walls and floor instills a feeling of unity. A 19th-
century Indian painting on cloth depicts a tiger.*

OPPOSITE: *In the Master Bath, a Braque lithograph strikes a muted chord, while a Picasso print graces the adjoining master bedroom.* ABOVE: *An airy Bedroom recalls 19th-century romanticism, with Near Eastern-style carpeting, Neo-Gothic architectural detailing and chairs in the style of Charles X. Black and white photographs are by Robert Demachy, the designer's grandfather, who was a pioneering photographer around the turn of the century.*

ALLURE OF PORTUGAL

There are many countries with climates equable enough to attract large expatriate communities. Far fewer boast local cultures that are rich enough to serve as a source of inspiration to their new residents. Portugal is a happy exception. It possesses both a lovely climate and a vigorous and prolific history. Even today it is still possible to speak of a Lusitanian world, stretching from Brazil to Macao. More unusual still is to find a new resident of an old country who is interested—and knowledgeable—enough to deal with its heritage. All these seemingly impossible juxtapositions were achieved, however, and the result is an impeccable and fully realized creation in Cascais, Portugal. Perhaps *collaboration* would be a better word, for few interior designers have enjoyed a more harmonious working relationship than that between Valerian Rybar and his discerning American client Mrs. Graham D. Mattison.

The calm and sturdy façade of a house modeled on the patrician country villas of eighteenth-century Portugal and set among pine trees serves as a reticent introduction to the use of the best resources in Portugal. "Ironically," says Mr. Rybar, "we have here one of the finest houses in the country. And it is, of course, new." With the help of French architect Pierre Barbe, Mr. Rybar planned the exterior of the house and took over the interior completely—executing a series of rooms that in their liveliness and international spirit are perfectly within the letter of Portuguese civilization, which has borrowed so gracefully from almost every part of the globe.

"There are several distinct motifs that run through the house," explains the designer. "They are all based squarely on Portuguese precedent. Wherever stone flooring is not used, for example, I specified polished brick. It looks superb, and it is wonderful to walk on. Then there is the use of tray ceilings. These

are simple vaults of wood painted white, although there are hundreds of ways to lay planking. The *azulejos*, which I use extensively throughout the house and in the pool pavilion, are, of course, the decorative tiles of Portugal, one of the most characteristic and important elements of decoration in this country. In fact, they have been used so overwhelmingly—particularly in the seventeenth and eighteenth centuries—that you might say that they form the basis of local ideas about decoration. And finally there are those beautiful pieces of furniture we found, not only in Portugal but in Italy and England too, which serve to complete the rooms." A mere listing of these elements, however, does little more than sketch the mood of the subtle balance the designer has successfully achieved between international luxury and national flavor.

"Here there is a great fund of skills that have almost died out elsewhere in Europe," continues Mr. Rybar. "Stonecutters, woodworkers, silversmiths and wrought-iron forgers, all of whose work is of the highest quality, were available. It was my challenge to use them sparingly. Everything is of the finest level of workmanship, and the whole house was executed with a degree of perfection perhaps unique under present conditions in the world today. Mrs. Mattison is a person who is attracted instinctively to perfection. And she understands that, in order to have a completely realized object of quality, this perfection must be carried out to the last detail."

To oversee the immense task of bringing her home to fruition, Mrs. Mattison tapped Valerian Rybar for his ability to invoke a unique and private universe. This talent is much in evidence throughout the house at Cascais, which is serious and amusing, sober and grand—a variation on ancient themes and an essay on the subject of living well.

63

PRECEDING PAGE: *The Cascais residence of Mrs. Graham D. Mattison is a modern interpretation of the country villas of 18th-century Portugal. Designer Valerian Rybar, with architect Pierre Barbe, used indigenous materials and the help of local craftsmen to flavor the structure with its heritage.* ABOVE: *The formal Entrance Hall includes an 18th-century Portuguese table and armchairs and a repoussé silver mirror.* RIGHT: *The contrast of dark woods against a pristine background lavish with architectural detail distinguishes the Library, a long room notable for its duplication of elements on each side. The Portuguese needlepoint rug and tray ceiling emphasize the strong linear quality of the design.*

In the Library, an intriguing symmetry
is achieved by the exacting placement of
paired furnishings: 18th-century Portuguese desk chairs and walnut secre-
taries, 17th-century English globes on
a Portuguese jacaranda table of the
same era, and Dutch brass chandeliers.

The strong contrast between light and dark elements continues in the Dining Room, where the patterning of the tray ceiling creates a pavilionlike effect. A large Dutch brass chandelier is suspended above the walnut table and 18th-century Portuguese chairs.

OPPOSITE: *Mrs. Mattison's Bedroom is a cheerful exposition of chinoiserie, with crisp lacquered Chippendale-style furnishings and screens detailed in Chinese motifs and fretwork. A Portuguese hand-stitched rug, concealing the polished antique brick flooring, adds color and vitality to the room.* ABOVE: *Mirrors reflect a pair of delicate antique ivory pagodas in Mrs. Mattison's oval-shaped Bath. The domed ceiling is painted to resemble a cloud-filled sky.*

ABOVE: *Traditional blue and white Portuguese tiles, called* azulejos, *cover the walls of the Pool Pavilion with a chinoiserie design in the manner of Jean Pillement. Rope tables and Victorian Gothic-style lacquered rattan chairs are played against the large-scale fantasy garden on the walls. Delectable fruits garnish the table settings of native stemware and porcelain plates.* RIGHT: *The swimming pool, lined in marbleized* azulejos, *mirrors the Pavilion.*

AMERICAN EMBASSY IN PARIS

To the delight of Americans and French alike, the American ambassador's residence in Paris underwent many changes when Ambassador Arthur Hartman and his wife, Donna, moved in. Before a transfer to the U.S. embassy in Moscow, they brought a relaxed style to the formal French diplomatic world. And they subtly changed the atmosphere of the residence itself by infusing a very Parisian *hôtel particulier* with American paintings, sculptures and folk arts and crafts. Early American quilts were used to embellish nineteenth-century paneled walls. A portrait of George Washington and an abstract artwork by Josef Albers were displayed overlooking a staircase designed by architect Ludovico Visconti for the original owner in the 1840s.

The embassy is a grand residence. Built by the baroness de Pontalba, an American who returned to the France of her ancestors, the three-story mansion occupies a large site on the rue du Faubourg Saint-Honoré, just one block from the Elysée Palace of the president of France. It was designed on a palatial scale by Visconti, who also designed Napoleon's Tomb. In 1876, Baron Edmond de Rothschild bought it, installing his vast collection of art, a good portion of which he eventually left to the Louvre when he died, in 1943. The Rothschilds made several alterations; all that remains of the original interior is the Visconti grand hall and staircase. In 1948 the house was sold to the U.S. government.

When she and her husband moved there, Mrs. Hartman was determined to make the embassy a reflection of American culture abroad. Her first decision was to take advantage of the Art in Embassies Program, which provides for American art to be lent to embassies around the world. She personally contacted museum curators, galleries and artists themselves, winning their cooperation with a combination of gentle persuasion and natural charm. She had a definite theme in mind: highlighting the French background in American art. Many of the artists represented, ranging from early American primitives to the most contemporary painters, had French ancestors. Others, like Albers, were Europeans who had settled in the United States, and still others had studied in France. "In presenting in our Paris residence a collection of American art, we had the feeling of having brought our friends with us," Ambassador and Mrs. Hartman say. "Our purpose was not to make a museum of our house, but to have with us witnesses to American civilization that our visitors could discover for themselves."

Although she moved quickly to have the artworks installed, Mrs. Hartman took her time in making major decorating changes. "I didn't want to move into a place that completely engulfed me and start making little changes here and there." Rather, she wanted to wait and observe how the house worked. Once this had been accomplished, the rooms were repainted, lightened and refurbished. Much old upholstery was replaced with less elaborate fabrics, and the lighting was made more flattering. Mrs. Hartman enjoyed creating flower arrangements, even for official functions. In winter, when the embassy gardens were not in bloom, she went to the wholesale flower market. Even with these changes, however, the mood of the house was preserved.

Under Hartman's tenure, the ambassador's residence was frequently used by the American community in Paris. Fund-raising events for charities were held here, and Ambassador and Mrs. Hartman were determined to open the doors as much as possible. "We wanted to let people use the embassy. We thought it should be used by—and for the benefit of—the wider American community."

The American Embassy in Paris, designed by Ludovico Visconti, was acquired by the United States in 1948. The former United States ambassador to France, Arthur Hartman, and his wife, Donna, brought new spirit to its noble halls. PRECEDING PAGE: *An imposing balance characterizes the embassy's south façade.* ABOVE: *In an octagonal Anteroom, visitors sign the embassy's* Livre d'or *register. Elie Nadelman's* Tango *was one of a collection of artworks borrowed by Mrs. Hartman for the residence.* RIGHT: *Woodwork from the home of 18th-century financier Samuel Bernard once graced the salon now named for him, used for formal embassy receptions. The original boiserie, deeded to a museum, was replaced by an exact copy in gesso. Two Cézanne paintings sparkle amid the stately exuberance.*

OPPOSITE: *An 18th-century Flemish tapestry animates the pastel-hued Dining Room, reserved for smaller receptions. The Sheraton table, which can accommodate three dozen guests, is set with crested china dinner service and crystal stemware.* ABOVE: *A grillwork monogram commemorates a former resident, the Baron Edmond de Rothschild.*

IN THE AUSTRIAN ALPS

The Tyrol is the land where edelweiss and purple violets bloom atop the tallest peaks, the chamois seeks the high ground in a vision of natural beauty, and far-off snowcapped mountains rise over the silvered blues and greens of cedar and spruce, pine and larch. This is a land where everything gleams in a flood of light. The name *Tyrol* is from the Illyrian word for "thoroughfare," but many have chosen to remain in this remote and enchanted place. Indeed, it offers a perfect retreat for the clients for whom interior designer Valerian Rybar has converted a hunting lodge into a year-round holiday house.

Though it has gone through many transformations, the exterior of the house still conveys a sense of the past. The twin towers were built in the early nineteenth century, and the original house and nearby hermitage are both out of the Middle Ages. "My aim was to 'de-hunting lodge' the home," says Mr. Rybar. "The owners wanted it to be as self-contained as possible, and as comfortable. Because it is so isolated, you have to be very self-sufficient." With this in mind, Mr. Rybar included a number of the most modern amenities—film projectors, a sophisticated sound system, game rooms, a large kitchen equipped with "all the gadgetry available for pleasant living," a gym and a sauna, among others.

"You can live on various levels in this house," says the designer. "One might be suitable for entertaining on a large scale, but another would be equally comfortable for the family alone." The great hall is the focus of the residence and it has held an audience of over 100 for concerts of classical music, while the adjoining eight-sided area—known simply as "The Octagon"—with its bar, television, stereo and banquettes, lends itself to rather more intimate family living. The outdoors is for skiing or trout fishing, hunting or hiking. Evenings, however, are for reading or music, writing or quiet conversation. All the civilized pleasures are present in full measure.

Although Mr. Rybar approached this project in a spirit of restoration, nothing really ever looked the way it does now. The great hall, with its rich walnut boiserie, in its earlier incarnation was a barn, its walls adorned with hunting trophies. The trophies have been taken down, and the area is now provided with splendid Renaissance furniture of a scale appropriate to so large a space. All that remains of the original décor is the eighteenth-century plasterwork on the dining room ceiling. If the sense of the past inside the lodge itself is something of an illusion, the sense of place is dramatically real. "I like to use as many local handicrafts and as much local labor as possible in the various houses I do," Mr. Rybar comments. The feeling of the Tyrol is evident in an extensive use of Austrian and Bavarian handicrafts, including wrought-iron lanterns and fixtures from Munich, and the warm walnut woodwork designed by Mr. Rybar and imported from northern Italy. But people in the Tyrol consider *that* local, too.

In the midst of such natural beauty, Valerian Rybar chose not to compete with the landscape. He limited his palette to white and beiges and browns, and details are at a minimum. "The windows with their spectacular views," he says, "are quite enough." Art and objets d'art, many of them bearing some historical relation to the estate itself, are of secondary importance. It is sufficient that each room evokes the past without fanfare and that a background has been created at once familiar and calm, conducive to the intellectual and social pursuits of the owners and their guests. In this luxurious but unobtrusive setting there is every opportunity to enjoy conversation, appreciate the works of mankind and acknowledge the greater works of nature.

PRECEDING PAGE: *Designer Valerian Rybar transformed a vast Tyrolean lodge into a year-round home. The original house dates from the Middle Ages.* OPPOSITE: *In the suede-wrapped Octagon, the tray ceiling molding and the lambrequin molding and tassels are of Italian walnut. Rodin bronzes rest on the center table. The 18th-century bas-relief portraits are German.* ABOVE: *Walnut and oak architectural detailing, Portuguese needlepoint rugs and a two-story library area define the Great Hall. Substantial furnishings include 17th-century Sienese armoires, Northern Italian Renaissance chairs and a refectory table*

81

Verdant color unifies the Dining Room, where German polychromed carved-wood chairs surround a Bavarian Baroque table. A naive 17th-century Tyrolean painting above the sideboard recalls the original house.

Inspired by a view of the surrounding forest, an intimate corner of the Library's upper level, appointed with a Northern Italian Renaissance desk and a brass lamp, encourages peaceful contemplation and study.

IN THE HEART OF PARIS

Among the most handsome streets in Paris, perhaps in the world, is the rue du Faubourg Saint-Honoré. On one side are fashionable shops, and on the other, through large doorways between stretches of high walls, can be seen the courtyards of some of the most beautiful eighteenth-century *hôtels particuliers* in Paris. In 1722 work began on one of the most graceful of them, the *Hôtel de Charost*, which is today the British Embassy. The property had been bought by the tutor to Louis XV, Paul François, duc de Charost, who was to become chief of the Royal Council of Finance and minister of the Council of State. In 1785, the duc de Charost, the original owner's grandson, rented the dwelling to a rich landowner from the Low Countries, the comte de la Marck, who undertook the completion of much of the eighteenth-century decoration still to be seen inside.

Then, in 1803, the townhouse was bought by the young woman who was to be its most flamboyant occupant: Napoleon's favorite and most beautiful sister, Pauline. She had just returned to Paris, a widow at twenty-three. Napoleon paid 300,000 francs of the 400,000-franc purchase price, and Pauline borrowed the rest, and more for decoration, from her brother Joseph and her sister Elisa. In less than a year she had discarded her widow's weeds, launched herself into elegant Parisian life and married again—this time a handsome Italian, Prince Borghese. She did not stay happily married for long, however, but continued her extravagant way of life, indulging in milk baths and often walking naked in front of her courtiers. She also posed, almost in the nude, for the sculptor Canova, and a small version of this famous sculpture can be seen in the embassy today. It was aptly said of the princess that, in the pursuit of pleasure, she "danced throughout the winter, took baths throughout the summer, and loved all the year round." During the eleven years she lived in the Hôtel de Charost—often called *le nid de Pauline*, "Pauline's nest"—she lavished money on it. Two large wings were added to the south side, facing the garden: The west wing was built to house the Borghese works of art; the east wing was to be the state dining room, which it remains to this day.

After Napoleon's abdication, in 1814, Pauline loyally joined him in exile on Elba. At the time, the duke of Wellington was instructed by the British government to find a permanent site for the embassy in Paris. As Pauline was short of funds, she sold the house and all its contents, except for the Borghese paintings, to the British government for the equivalent of £275,000. Wellington lived in the newly acquired British Embassy for only five months, although he later returned to Paris as a delegate to the post-Waterloo peace conference. During his short stay, however, he entertained lavishly, sparing no expense on new silver and Sèvres china for the grand house in order to maintain its prestige.

Although more than two centuries have passed since the first description of the Hôtel de Charost was written in the archives of the Seine, the basic plan of the residence has been changed very little. Some rooms have been added, but the grand suite on the ground floor still contains the state rooms, used for entertaining dignitaries. The first floor, with its series of lofty rooms, is still reserved for day-to-day living. Possibly the best description of the mansion was made by Sir Duff Cooper, one of the British ambassadors who left his mark on the Hôtel de Charost. In his memoirs he wrote: "Part of the regret with which I left the embassy was due to the fondness I had come to feel for the house. I sometimes felt it was haunted by spirits of the pleasant people who had sat in its comfortable rooms."

PRECEDING PAGE: *The Hôtel de Charost was once the residence of Napoleon's sister Pauline. Since 1814, it has served as the British Embassy in Paris.* OPPOSITE ABOVE: *Pauline updated the Salon Or et Blanc with Empire flourishes. A model of a Canova sculpture depicts her as Venus. The portrait is by Kinsoen.* OPPOSITE: *The Gallery was added in 1826.* ABOVE: *The Library was formerly the bedroom of Prince Borghese. The desk once belonged to the duke of Wellington.*

ABOVE: *Originally constructed by Pauline to house the Borghese art collection, the Ballroom was completely redecorated on the occasion of Queen Victoria's state visit in 1855.*
OPPOSITE ABOVE: *The Queen's Bedroom reflects* le style anglais *of the 19th century.*
OPPOSITE: *In Pauline's Bedroom is the lavishly draped* lit de parade *from which she liked to receive visitors. An octagonal Empire dressing mirror bears candles for illumination. Pauline added the Empire fabrics.*

ANCIENT ITALIAN FORTRESS

In the serene, almost Flemish countryside near Parma, where the drama of the Italian landscape subsides before the climax of the Alps, lies *La Rocca di Soragna*, home of Prince Bonifazio Meli Lupi. Not only has the castle been a family possession for over a thousand years but, since its restoration in the seventeenth century, generations of Meli Lupi princes have endowed it with a sumptuous array of interiors. The grand styles of Italian mural painting and domestic decoration, from late Renaissance to the time of the Gothic revival, are all to be found here. The present owner, Don Bonifazio III, is a direct descendant of this ancient line. Still regarded by the community as their feudal lord, the prince has done notable work in improving agriculture and reconstructing farmhouses in this region of Emilia.

Outwardly the castle has changed very little. Spare of classical elements, the façade has the decorous austerity that is a hallmark of ducal Parma, just twenty miles to the east. But inside the courtyard, the curtain goes up on Renaissance spectacle with great splendor. Carlo Draghi's triumphal staircase, with its red Verona marble balusters and sporting *putti*, is a magnificent introduction to the Great Gallery on the upper floor, where Francesco and Ferdinando Bibiena, star artists of the late-seventeenth-century Emilian school of theatrical perspective, frescoed a vast frame of architectonic trompe l'oeil interset with medallions, representing tableaux of the history of the Meli Lupi family. The Bibienas were considered the greatest designers for the opera stage in theatrical history, and the square stuccoed room on the ground floor is an explosion of their pyrotechnics. The paintings, allegorical glorifications of the Meli Lupis routing the Turks, appear through a massive framework of stucco moldings, covering the walls and ceiling in their entirety.

Beyond the Great Gallery, the Room of Strong Women—frescoed in 1702 by Bolla and Clerici in collaboration with the Bibienas—brings the spectacle to a climax. The two principal tableaux show Judith and Jael, each dispatching her man: Jael, in a picturesquely heroic pose, hammers a nail through the brain of Sisera while on the adjacent wall Judith demurely clutches the dripping head of Holofernes. The room at one time functioned as an antechamber of the gilded Throne Room next door, and the scenes were no doubt intended to send a shiver of apprehension down the spine of the most hardened petitioner. The Throne Room and Nuptial Chamber are built for more serious matters. Here the ornamentation is mostly confined to exquisitely carved gilded wood, another specialty of Emilian Baroque in the early eighteenth century. To the left of the bed is a small sitting room with an inlaid polychrome marble floor bearing the heraldic figures of the family crest. It is the only marble floor in the castle.

The Long Gallery of 1798, extending 200 feet into the park, bridges the eighteenth and nineteenth centuries. Decorated with pastoral scenes deriving from Classical and Renaissance poets, the gallery ends in a pavilion opening onto the terrace of a tower and a small wooded lake. Viewed from the garden, this is perhaps the most enchanting aspect of the English Park, designed by Voghera in the early nineteenth century. The few acres of ground surrounding the castle have been ingeniously exploited by the disposition of thickets, lake and hills to conjure up the illusion of miles of uninterrupted woodland populated by occasional Baroque statues, survivors of the seventeenth-century Italian garden. The Rocca di Soragna, a fortress and the scene of past violence, is now a peaceful home and museum—and a record of centuries of art and history.

91

PRECEDING PAGE: *The countryside west of Parma provides the setting for the imposing Rocca di Soragna, the historic residence of the Meli Lupi dynasty.* ABOVE: *The set of six original 16th-century frescoes, in the Sala del Baglione, are by Cesare Baglione of Cremona.* OPPOSITE: *In the Grande Galleria, 17th-century artists Francesco and Ferdinando Bibiena frescoed tableaux that record events in the lives of the Meli Lupis. The painted framework exemplifies the Emilian Baroque technique of architectural trompe l'oeil.*

PRECEDING PAGES: *Tableaux representing feminine heroism in biblical times command the Sala delle Donne Forti, antechamber of the throne room. The frescoes were created in 1702 by Giovanni Bolla and Giovanni Leonardo Clerici.* ABOVE: *The frescoes in the Piccola Galleria Secentesca, by Francesco Bibiena, one of the great set designers for opera, are a rare instance of a Baroque artist's re-creating the styles of three generations earlier.*

LEFT: *Paintings by Giulio Campi and Il Parmigiano were taken from another floor and remounted in the Sala del Campi. Above the fireplace is Il Parmigiano's* Love Fitting an Arrow into His Bow. BELOW: *In the Sala del Trono, a carved and gold-leafed Baroque baldachin overhangs the throne. The walls are covered in Genoa velvet and brocade.*

ABOVE: *Within the ornate alcove of the Camera Nuziale, a baldachin draped in silk-embroidered Genoa velvet extends over the marriage bed; a sculpted and gold-leafed railing encloses the space. Brocade-and-velvet-upholstered walls backdrop a Murano mirror framed in inlaid and painted crystal.*

OPPOSITE: *The wooden walls and ceiling of the Salottino are richly carved and gilded, framing three family portraits. The inlaid polychrome marble floor, bearing the heraldic figures of the family crest, is the only marble floor to be found in the castle.*

VILLA AT CAP FERRAT

Monte Carlo has changed since the days when it was celebrated in light opera and films. But its fabled past endures in the glittering casino and the *Belle Epoque* hotels, triumphs of Edwardian pomp; and the villas that bejewel nearby Cap d'Ail and Cap Ferrat, in France, still inspire the imagination. These were once the residences of grand dukes, ballet stars, English milords and, presumably, the man who broke the bank and was immortalized in song. Not long ago, interior designer Lorenzo Mongiardino created the interiors for such a villa, a late-nineteenth-century structure overlooking the edge of Cap Ferrat, where sheer cliffs drop abruptly to a sea the color of sapphires. The villa was designed in the eclectic Neo-Classical style of the period, with porticoed verandas, elaborate architectural detailing, glassed double doors and opulent mirrors.

Fortunately, the architecture remained intact through a succession of owners. During the 1960s, an internationally famous Pop group moved in and, indeed, rocked the villa to its foundations, leaving it in a sorry state. The next resident had the floors, plumbing and wiring redone, the interiors painted white, and modern furnishings installed. Finally, the villa was sold to a young woman who was looking for a year-round home near Monte Carlo for herself and her two children. She loved the villa, the surrounding garden, the views toward the sea. As time passed, however, she became uncomfortable with the modern décor. Feeling that a change was needed, she called Lorenzo Mongiardino in Milan. Together, the designer and the new resident decided that the mansion should be restored to reflect the great days of Monte Carlo and the Côte d'Azur.

Most important, it was to be a home, not a lifeless period re-creation. In addition, as Lorenzo Mongiardino explains: "Since the Edwardian era is associated with grand hotels, I was particularly concerned with avoiding the look of a hotel. To be safe, I took it back one step further and gave it a late-Victorian emphasis. For color tones, I took into account the three important collections in the house: the Charles X furniture, the handsome celadon vases and the varied set of blue and white bowls and plates." For the living room, the designer fashioned simple cube tables that incorporate marquetry of light and dark woods, echoing the inlaid Charles X furniture. Augmenting these furnishings is seating upholstered in velours, including a pouf that seems to be the perfect prop for cultivated discussion in the Edwardian manner. The appointments are scaled low, accentuating the spaciousness of the room.

A typical Mongiardino touch is the extensive use of wallpaper—in the living room, sitting room, library and elsewhere. In fact, it is only in the dining room that *papier peint* is replaced, by panels of Indian-style Italian-made cotton that serve as delicate Oriental backgrounds for blue and white plates. The wallpapers date back to the late nineteenth century. Signor Mongiardino discovered them in a shop in Genoa—leftovers that seemed to have outlived their vogue. "I've been buying up these old papers for years," says the designer. "Now I have quite a collection to draw on for the right houses."

The tonal nuances of the architectural detailing, and the various complementary patterns of flooring, rugs and upholstery fabrics, come together in remarkable harmony. Recalling the Edwardian flair for deftly understated pattern-on-pattern, this harmony and the plush comfort of the décor offer a contrast to the asceticism of much modern design. As transformed by Lorenzo Mongiardino, this villa at Cap Ferrat gently reaffirms the continued appeal of the *Belle Epoque* and of the Côte d'Azur.

*Lorenzo Mongiardino's interior designs
for a villa in Cap Ferrat recall the
Belle-Epoque elegance of the Côte
d'Azur.* PRECEDING PAGE: *Balustrades
edge the roof, balconies and verandas of
the late-19th-century residence.*

ABOVE AND RIGHT: *The Louis XV boiserie distinguishing
the Living Room creates tonal resonances with a selection of
antique celadon porcelains. Panels of late-19th-century
German wallpaper reinforce the color scheme with a flour-
ish of pattern. The inlaid cube tables were designed to complement the Charles X furniture, including chairs that
punctuate the ample windows. A large, well-cushioned
pouf occupies the center of the room, while an 18th-
century Venetian glass chandelier sparkles from above.*

The Dining Room contains a collection of antique blue and white porcelain objets. A 19th-century Persian rug overlays the interlinked pattern of parquet flooring. The antique English mahogany table, chairs and console lend contrast to the light tones that prevail. Adding to the Oriental influence are wall panels of Indian-style cotton. An antique crystal chandelier and subtly colored architectural detailing highlight the ensemble with modulations of light and hue.

RIGHT: Faux-bois *wallpaper was darkened to harmonize with the furnishings in the Library. Reflected in the mirror are works by de Chirico, Sassu, Campigli and Rosai.* BELOW RIGHT: *Early-18th-century works by Cignaroli and 19th-century architectural paintings in oval frames add interest to the Stairwell.* OPPOSITE: *In the Master Bedroom, checkered and solid silk taffeta, a quilted silk bedcovering, and pillows covered in Indian fabrics offer subtle variations of texture, pattern and color.*

A MAHARAJA'S PALACE

The British Raj in India may have gone with a whimper, but some of the Indian princes made more spectacular exits. Right through the 1930s and 1940s, the maharaja of Jodhpur was engaged in building a colossal new palace that rivaled *Viceroy's House* in New Delhi in size. Its well-preserved interior presents a great number of astonishing examples of the decorative styles of the early 1930s.

Jodhpur was the old principality of Marwar, one of the Hindu Rajput states whose rulers retained their independence under British dominion. The stability imposed by the British Raj allowed them to accumulate immense wealth. Many of them, influenced by British ideas of civilization and progress, spent their fortunes on modernizing their states as well as on themselves, combining an enthusiasm for the latest fashions and inventions of the West with all the pomp and splendor of Oriental potentates.

One such ruler was Maharaja Sir Umaid Singh, who undertook to build his new palace in 1929 as part of a public works program to relieve the distress caused by famine. A site was selected on Chittar Hill, an outcrop of rock 100 feet high, southeast of the old city. Tradition demanded that the palace be placed on the highest point of the hill, despite the difficulties this imposed. Soil for the gardens had to be brought up and the rock broken by blasting to give root space for the trees. A narrow-gauge railway was put down to bring in the Sussagar sandstone, and a landing field for aircraft was laid out.

The maharaja's English architects were Messrs. Lanchester and Lodge, with G. A. Goldstraw as resident architect. Lanchester had a considerable practice in India, both as architect and town planner. In 1912 he sat on the commission that advised on the siting of the new capital of New Delhi; he also designed the United Provinces Council Chamber building in Lucknow and Calcutta's Birkmyre Hotel. His plan for the *Umaid Bhavan Palace* is symmetrical, in the Beaux-Arts tradition. North of the domed circular halls is the staff court; to the south, the *zenana*, or women's court. The dome dominates the composition, but around it are flanking towers that create a romantic skyline and do much to relieve the building's vast bulk. Its monumental, crisply cut stone façades have a quality that is most impressive.

However, the usual Anglo-Indian "Indo-Saracenic" manner of building was not chosen. Since the region had not been long under Muslim domination, a Hindu style was selected by the architects. But the style is not typical of Indian buildings for it is applied to a system of articulation that is clearly Classical. The design is indebted to Viceroy's House in New Delhi, designed by Sir Edwin Landseer Lutyens, but Lanchester had none of Lutyens's skill in fusing East and West. Here the Oriental detail is applied, not integrated into the architecture itself. The maharaja turned to another firm for the decoration of some rooms. Many of the private and guest suites reflect still another aspect of the 1920s and 1930s, with Art Déco and Streamline Moderne furnishings.

Alas, the interiors were never finished. World War II interrupted shipments from Britain, and the remainder of the furnishings were destroyed. Maharaja Sir Umaid Singh died, and by 1950 the heady days of palace building were over. An independent India had little love for princely display. The Umaid Bhavan was used as administrative offices; now it is a hotel, with the present maharaja living in one wing. Declining fortunes, however, have not affected its appearance. There is none of that poignant decay evident in many Indian palaces. In its gracious perfection, the Umaid Bhavan stands as a stately reminder of the grandeur of the past.

Rising from the austere semiarid landscape of Rajasthan, the Umaid Bhavan Palace, residence of the maharaja of Jodhpur, evokes memories of the halcyon days of the British Raj. PRECEDING PAGE: *Designed by English architects and begun in 1929, the romantic structure atop an outcropping of rock near Jodhpur exhibits an essentially classical form with applied Hindu details.* LEFT: *Beneath a great dome, the circular Central Hall serves as the architectural focus of the vast, symmetrically organized building. At once opulent and severe, the stone rotunda resembles both the apse of a cathedral and the central court of a mosque.* ABOVE: *The Beaux-Arts character of the design is reinforced by the oval grand staircase adjoining the Central Hall.*

111

LEFT: *The streamlined curvilinear forms in the reception area of a Guest Suite were inspired by the luxury ocean liners; their popularity paralleled the conception of this last great Indian palace. Polish designer S. Norblin executed the colorful stylized painting. Hanwant Singh, heir apparent at the time, collaborated with Norblin on the décor.* ABOVE: *The Throne Room indicates that Eastern tradition, as well as Western innovation, was lavishly served. The symbolic paintings are also by S. Norblin.*

113

RIGHT AND BELOW: *Sumptuous in its simplicity, a Guest Bath is richly veneered in onyx and marble and shaped with curving mirrored niches and sleek Art Déco fittings; wall sconces with indirect lighting were recent inventions at that time.* OPPOSITE: *A chrome-banded bed, in the style of Emile Ruhlmann, rests on a curved platform in a Guest Room. An acid-etched black glass fantasy by S. Norblin provides a dramatic backdrop.*

IN THE TUSCAN STYLE

Incredibly enough, there are corners in Tuscany today that have remained almost as they were in the days of the Medici. There are still landscapes that appeared as backgrounds in the portraits of the Cinquecento masters: scenes of olive-clad hills laced with vines and punctuated by black cypresses; here a cloister and there a ruined tower standing stark against the sky. In such a setting, in the hills above Florence, stands the *Villa delle Rose,* a nobly proportioned house of the classical Tuscan style, which in 1958 was discovered in a state of near ruin by the Ernest Boissevains. An American couple—she was Jean Tennyson, of opera fame—they came upon the property, fell in love with it, bought it and spent the next four years bringing it back to life.

The villa's origins lie hidden in obscurity, as very few documents have survived. It is known, however, that in the fifteenth century it was a fortified farm, and that in 1487 Nicolo Antinori, a Tuscan nobleman, purchased it with the idea of converting it into a modern dwelling. With this in mind, he penned the following suggestions for his architect: "It should be just large enough for me, my family and a few friends. Think about a garden and a little ground to cultivate." Succeeding generations of the Antinori family continued to enhance and develop the property, making it a masterpiece of its kind. This happy state of affairs was brought to a rude halt by the outbreak of World War II. During the next four years the villa was occupied by a succession of military forces: first the Germans, and then the Americans. Officers were billeted in the house, while soldiers pitched their tents in the fields. The ballroom was transformed into the officers' mess.

"When we found the villa," says Mr. Boissevain, "it was a wreck. The roof leaked; one of the columns of the loggia had crumbled, and the courtyard was a sea of mud." The new owners chose Count Niccolo Rucellai, a Florentine architect specializing in the restoration of antique buildings, to oversee the work of reconstruction, in cooperation with the Belle Arti, the Italian government's fine arts commission. In the process certain architectural elements that had been altered during the preceding century were restored to their original size and form.

In the reception rooms the major impact of décor has been rightly left to the frescoes. For this reason, much else is neutral: beige carpeting covers the floors, and solid-colored fabrics were used for drapery and upholstery. Indicating a Baroque console in one of the salons, Mrs. Boissevain says: "At first, I put quite a few pieces of this kind in the house, but I soon took them out again. They were just too much." She replaced several elaborately carved tables with simple antique Chinese ones, and they suit the rooms admirably. The Boissevains made practical use of odd-sized spaces. "One curious feature of this house is the tiny rooms between the ground floor and the upper floor. They were originally maids' rooms, but we use them for offices."

Across the courtyard, facing the loggia, are the oldest buildings in the complex: the tower, the library and the chapel. The Boissevains had the tower gutted, and then divided the space into a number of guest rooms. The topmost floor was converted into a studio, where both husband and wife work at sculpture. The upper floor of the main house, which was the granary in the original farmhouse, has been redesigned to contain the private suite of the owners as well as additional guest rooms and baths. From here, panoramic views reach far into the countryside. Looking out over this landscape, "listening" to the silence, who would really believe that bustling Florence lies so very near?

Time had ravaged the 15th-century Tuscan Villa delle
Rose when it was discovered by Mr. and Mrs. Ernest Boissevain, in 1958. Patient restoration revived its classic beauty.
PRECEDING PAGE: An archway framing the main en-
trance emphasizes the classical detailing of the residence and
its harmonious proportions. ABOVE: The villa is named for
the roses that grow luxuriantly in the surrounding gardens.
Broad lawns and cypress trees enhance its beauty. RIGHT:
In the Grand Salon, late-18th-century frescoes are a theatrical
mix of trompe l'oeil architectural elements and panoramas.
Silk-damask-upholstered furniture adds warmth. A
Quentin Massys Madonna and Child adorns the grand piano.

LEFT: *Mythical scenes, a trompe l'oeil dado and a doorway molding painted to resemble carved stone create an ornate background for the large Dining Room. A richly patterned Aubusson rug and a contrastingly fragile Venetian chandelier complete the effect. The furnishings include Louis XIV Italian chairs and a 16th-century table.* ABOVE: *The frescoes in the smaller Dining Room are an airy, intricate blend of Herculaneum-inspired figural images and decorative motifs.*

121

LEFT: *The distinction between reality and illusion becomes less clear in the galleried Ballroom/Reception Hall, where Italian Baroque carved-wood sculptures intermingle with trompe l'oeil statuary.* ABOVE: *In the State Bedroom, trompe l'oeil architectural detailing complements an ornate appliquéd bedcovering, canopy and illusionist headboard.*

123

MOROCCAN SPLENDOR

The view from the tower of the *Villa Taylor* sets the scene. The forest of cypresses and olives in the park below seems to obliterate both the old and the new parts of Marrakech. But from the tower the view extends across the dusty cemetery to the stout pink gateway of the old city and opens onto a welter of *souks* and minarets. Behind the ancient gate are stalls offering copper and leather; resplendently dyed loops of wool; whiffs of cinnamon and camphor; bales of fresh muslin and hemp. And also mud, donkeys, tar, and fumes from rusty automobiles.

The Villa Taylor itself is a paradox. Known to the locals as the "American villa," it turns an amusing volte-face on the course of twentieth-century *moeurs*: It was built by an American millionairess in the 1920s, only to be purchased after World War II by one of the most ancient and noble families of France. The present owner is the comtesse de Breteuil, and here she has lived since 1947. By that year the villa had already acquired a distinguished history. It was built between 1923 and 1926 by Mrs. Moises Taylor, a granddaughter of President Ulysses S. Grant, as an occasional winter retreat. The good times ended in the 1930s, however, and the house was virtually deserted until the outbreak of war, when it became the American Headquarters in Morocco. It was at the Villa Taylor that Churchill and Roosevelt stayed after the Casablanca Conference in 1942–1943.

After the war, the comte de Breteuil's mother bought the villa in 1947 and presented it to her son and his bride. And ever since Villa Taylor has been a hub of social life for all distinguished visitors to Morocco. A widow, the countess has lived alone in the Villa Taylor since the death of her son, but her shy charm and elegance, as well as her dazzling guest list of international celebrities, keep the house filled with life. The countess says that she does not really miss Paris, though once a year she returns to France or Italy for a month. The vast and stately *Château de Breteuil* at Chevreuse, just outside of Paris, is run by her nephew, and all her own family furniture that she has no use for in Morocco is there. The collections of paintings and furniture the de Breteuils did bring from Paris have settled down perfectly in an atmosphere of Moorish arches, arabesque mosaics, carved inlaid panels and the splash of fountains in the elaborately tiled courts.

Comtesse de Breteuil's real passion is for her garden. On the drive up from the gates, the overbranching olives and clumps of cypress, the clusters of cannas hugging the irrigation canals, the flowering thickets all bespeak the verdant landscape of France. Behind the house great banks of northern blooms—hollyhocks, stocks, snapdragons, poppies and gigantic roses like crimson sunbursts—fling broad splashes of color against the tall gray grasses, spiky succulents and patches of bare pink soil. But there are enough large palms surrounding the villa and pool areas—with their cushions, their tiles and their draped divans—to keep the scene anchored in the desert south of the Mediterranean.

It is easy to see why Europe has lost its attractiveness for the countess in light of the way of life at Villa Taylor. Since the de Breteuils established themselves in Marrakech, a growing number of Americans and eminent Europeans have settled here. Names such as Getty, Krupp and Yves Saint-Laurent—a very close friend of the comtesse de Breteuil—are now well known in Marrakech. This pink city in the desert has become the most brilliant outpost of an older civilization where the values that go with leisure, tolerance and fine living can be respected, without the lurches and spills of social change now buckling the great cities of Europe.

The imposing three-story Villa Taylor, built between 1924 and 1926 for the granddaughter of President Ulysses S. Grant, was acquired in 1947 by the de Breteuil family. PRECEDING PAGE: *The view from the tower includes a courtyard of marble tiles, tall palms and trickling fountains.* OPPOSITE: *The Main Drawing Room exemplifies the traditional Moroccan architecture of the villa. The pierced wooden screen above the alcove masks a cozy mezzanine. The 18th-century portrait is of Gabrielle Emilie de Breteuil, mistress of the French philosopher Voltaire.* ABOVE: *Art Déco elements in the Dining Room were added in 1926.*

Fascinating and intricate mosaic tilework covers a Guest Room wall. The ceiling is of carved and inlaid wood. A Moroccan architect designed the villa, and craftsmen from Marrakech and Fez executed the architectural decoration.

ABOVE RIGHT: *A painted arabesque fantasy enriches the plaster walls of a tower Bedroom. The carved tables and chairs, the leather-covered pouf and the rug are Moroccan.* RIGHT: *The view from the drawing room encompasses a tiled swimming pool and the distinctive Islamic façade of the tower.*

AN EIGHTEENTH-CENTURY FOLLY

Although the *Menagerie* has been called a folly, its character and its function set it apart from most of the towers, obelisks and mock ruins with which eighteenth-century English landowners were wont to adorn their parks. Unlike so many follies that were designed by amateurs and inexpensively built, the Menagerie is the solid work of an established architect, Thomas Wright, of Durham. It is a handsome stone building in the Palladian style, finely detailed and well wrought, standing on the grounds of *Horton House*. Demolished in the 1930s, Horton House was the ancestral home of the earls of Halifax. It was the second earl who, around 1754, commissioned the Menagerie. As its name implies, the Menagerie was intended to be the adjunct to a small zoo. Here, according to Horace Walpole in 1763, his lordship had assembled "two young tigers," storks, raccoons, an eagle, "hogs from the Havannah with navels on their backs" and "many basons of gold fish." To enjoy this bizarre collection, the earl brought his guests to the Menagerie, often entertaining them in the sumptuous dining room.

Two hundred years later this distinguished building was totally derelict. When Gervase Jackson-Stops, the present owner, bought it in 1973, the roofs on the end pavilions and the lead dome over the bay window had been stripped off; windows were boarded up; none of the original sashes remained. In the dining room, where the cream of eighteenth-century society had passed so many pleasant hours, hay was heaped as high as the cornices, and the plasterwork was in a very bad way. Gervase Jackson-Stops is one of England's leading art historians and architectural conservationists. With the help of his mother, an architect, he set about to restore the building and to adapt it, with suitable additions, to twentieth-century living.

The most important task of restoration was to reconstitute the missing or damaged plasterwork in the one-time dining room, now the living room. Luckily, some old photographs existed. Working from these, Mr. Jackson-Stops, along with artist Christopher Hobbs, succeeded in wholly restoring the decorations. By referring to paintwork found in dark corners, they returned the walls and ceiling to their former tones, so that today the room exhibits all its original features and glows with the colors of its heyday. Where there were no photographs to work from, they had to improvise. One day they were congratulating themselves on having devised a particularly fine design of swags, lyres and ribbons when, to their delight, a local farmer dropped in and said something to the effect that it was quite lovely, but not quite like the original! In former times, he and his dog had spent long hours in the ruin, sheltering from the rain. Many years later the farmer could still recall the decorative motifs perfectly.

The modern additions to the folly evolved naturally from the plan of the Menagerie. This comprised a central block containing the dining room with a kitchen underneath, linked by screen walls to two flanking pavilions. These elements formed the impressive front elevation of the house as seen from across the lake. The back elevation, which was all the young tigers saw, had—and still has—an unfinished look about it. By enclosing the area behind the screen walls, and keeping below screen level, Mr. Jackson-Stops has provided extra accommodation in the wings without impairing the front elevation or spoiling the rear one. The state to which the Menagerie had deteriorated would have put off all but the most sanguine purchaser, which Mr. Jackson-Stops most firmly was. As a result, he has preserved exquisitely a miniature architectural gem.

PRECEDING PAGE: *The Menagerie was commissioned circa 1754 as an adjunct to a private zoo on the grounds of Horton House, in Northampton, the ancestral home of the earls of Halifax. The Palladian-style building was acquired in 1973 by Gervase Jackson-Stops, who restored its architectural detailing and adapted it to 20th-century living.* ABOVE: *The near façade was built of brick rather than stone, reflecting the fact that 18th-century "eye-catchers" were meant to be seen only from the front.* OPPOSITE: *Old photographs and existing detailing guided the restoration of the central pavilion, now the Living Room. The bronze urn is a replica based on a description by Horace Walpole, who visited the Menagerie in 1763.*

OPPOSITE: *Added behind the west screen wall, the present Dining Room evokes the mood of ease characteristic of English country houses. Antique furnishings include the French Empire commode, a fall-front desk and oak dining chairs. Above a mid-18th-century mahogany chair, botanical plates encircle a tôle wall sconce.* ABOVE: *Establishing a period flavor in the Master Bedroom are the festooned draperies above the French doors, a marble-topped French commode and a japanned armchair.*

RENAISSANCE VILLA REVITALIZED

Roman traffic surges up the via Veneto and down alongside the Villa Borghese. There, almost at a right angle to the entrance of the museum, stands the Brachetti-Peretti house, a tall building whose façade is embedded in a grandiose stone structure. The building's core is based on designs by a master architect of the Renaissance, Giacomo Barozzi.

Four hundred years ago, a house like this, outside the ancient Roman walls, was in the open country. The original villa was erected as a country retreat for Cardinal Giovanni Battista Pallotta (1594–1668), and so it acquired the name it bears today: *Grotta Pallotta*. Its fields and vineyards once stretched as far as the via Salaria. Today they lie buried beneath city streets. A succession of cardinals acquired Pallotta's villa, but it was not until the French cardinal Alfonse Hubert de Latier took possession in the mid-eighteenth century that it was expanded and embellished to proportions far more noble than those of its earlier use. After that, there were no further alterations made until early in the twentieth century, when architect Carlo Maria Busiri-Vici added an upper floor and extended the building along the via Pinciana.

This was the house that Count and Countess Brachetti-Peretti bought in the early 1970s. The young couple are keen on decorating and painting. Indeed, an artistic flair runs in the family, and the countess's sister, Elsa Peretti, has had enormous success in designing jewelry. "The place was in rather a bad way when we bought it," says the count, "so there was a good deal to do. But I wanted to do everything myself—all the decoration, that is. The architectural work was done by Patrizio Busiri-Vici."

Few European cities pose the challenges of redecoration that Rome does. The owner of a historic house cannot simply renovate it. Permission must first be granted by the Superintendent of Monuments and the City Council, and the historical character of the house must be rigorously preserved.

Within the parameters set forth by law, and the owners' desire to create a somewhat contemporary environment, the house resolves itself into three main areas: the entrance and white salons; the historic frescoed drawing room and anteroom, and the upstairs apartments. Downstairs, the sitting rooms and salons rely on Baroque proportions and vaulted ceilings to create an air of magnificence. The furniture, much of it Venetian, from the count's ancestral home, is eighteenth century. The frescoes, however, are the most splendid features in the house. There are trompe l'oeil colonnades, the courtly swirl of *putti*, garlands and architectural devices of old. The upstairs, where most of the family life goes on, is frankly contemporary. Terraces let in the sun, and the *altana* a floor higher provides a spot for pleasant summer meals. In these less formal quarters the art represents the count and countess's personal tastes: sculpture by Cascella and Trubbiani, paintings by Lucio Fontana, Dorazio and Capogrossi—all Italian contemporaries. And yet there are also eighteenth-century pieces: polychrome Venetian mirrors, a Roman writing table, a French *dormeuse* in the master bedroom, and leather-covered Louis XVI chairs.

Below the balconies the garden extends to a well-cut English lawn and then is lost in pines and holm oaks. Roman columns slumber in the grass; like the marble column inside the house, they have never left the premises since they first were raised 2,000 years ago. Was the place a Roman villa devastated in an age when Aurelian's city walls were used to keep the invaders at bay? Whatever the facts, the ancient foundations are still to be seen. Cardinal Pallotta first resurrected the villa, and today's house is still another phoenix rising from the imperial ashes.

LEFT: *In the Main Salon, 18th-century modifications introduced elaborate trompe l'oeil frescoes and a lacunar ceiling attributed to French artist Jean Le Pautre. A simplified seating arrangement provides a modern contrast to the surrounding splendor and an Aubusson rug.* ABOVE: *Neo-Classical frescoes lend aureate mellowness to the Small Salon, illuminated by a Venetian chandelier. Late-18th-century appointments include a Roman marble-topped table and a lacquered Piedmontese bench and chairs.*

139

More contemporary in its elegance is a Salon crowned by a vaulted ceiling. Light-toned walls, draperies and upholstery enhance the deep walnut of an 18th-century secretary. The table at the center of the seating arrangement bears a collection of delicate objects. The four small paintings are by the 18th-century Venetian artist Francesco Guardi.

TOP: *In the Hall between the vaulted salon and the dining room, two early-18th-century copper engravings by Vasi depict St. Peter's Basilica.* ABOVE: *The dramatic darkness of the Dining Room sets off the porcelain dinner service. The columnar sculpture is by Arnaldo Pomodoro. Vitrines display a generous collection of 18th-century china.*

ABOVE: *Lofty trees and a sweep of lawn contribute to the garden's parklike character.* TOP AND OPPOSITE: *Antique Roman cobblestone flooring in the Gazebo and a pair of ancient marble columns create a suitably classic setting for the azure pool. The gazebo provides an inviting shelter for dining surrounded by the beauty of the garden.*

142

BAROQUE GRANDEUR IN BRITAIN

Nearly three centuries old, *Castle Howard*, perhaps Britain's greatest Baroque palace, rises superbly from magnificent parkland surrounds. The huge dome—the first ever built in this kingdom—is surmounted by a gilded lantern that glitters in the sun. A design of lakes with vast oaks and beeches adorns the man-made landscape, rich with its Temple of the Four Winds, Doric mausoleum and other architectural extravaganzas. The heroic interior of the castle, of golden limestone, is galleried, pillared and arched, with vaulted ceilings—a splendor of perspectives. King Charles II found Saint Paul's Cathedral "awe-full," but somehow Castle Howard never overawes. Mr. George Howard, eighth Howard of Castle Howard, says it is the subtle difference between the appeal of Leningrad and the cold grandeur of Moscow. Perhaps it is a perfection in proportion that softens the impact of sheer size.

Castle Howard was not merely the first and most shining achievement of soldier-turned-architect John Vanbrugh. It was also the joint concept and endeavor of a triumvirate: Vanbrugh; Nicholas Hawksmoor, who had been trained by the Royal Architect, Wren; and Charles Howard, third earl of Carlisle. The earl certainly would have respected the work of Christopher Wren, and he knew the immensely popular Vanbrugh, approving his talent and originality of design. But what a brave decision to give the architect his support in a first unproved venture on such a scale! Who cannot imagine his relief at securing the tough professionalism of Hawksmoor to bring the flowing sketches to a state of stone and mortar? In short, Lord Carlisle knew exactly what he wanted. He was in the mood to build, and, as Acting Earl Marshal of England, he understood both parade and grandeur. Vanbrugh was the toast of the town; Baroque was in the air.

Throughout the years successive owners added to the palace's luster. The fourth earl, who amassed an astonishing array of classical and Egyptian sculpture, had lived in Rome, and Castle Howard received his great additions as if built for them. Even Mr. Howard looked uncertain when asked what on earth could have filled his palace before the statuary arrived! The fourth earl also set out to complete Vanbrugh's original plan for the west wing, using his brother-in-law, Sir Thomas Robinson, as architect. George Howard, in his turn, rebuilt the dome destroyed by fire in 1940, enlarged the collections of his forebears with Bow porcelain figures and Henry Moore and Rodin bronzes, and assembled an extensive array of historic costumes. He also planned an Old English rose garden in memory of his late wife, daughter of the duke of Grafton, and maintains his house with devoted care. He has added new sections to the splendid carved wood cornices, and painstakingly revives original hangings. Particularly fine are the eighteenth-century curtains of the bed used by the visiting Queen Victoria, refurbished so that the decoration peers through the transparent net.

So George Howard, even as his ancestors, restores and renews in a way that unites past and present and launches them both into the future in happy unity. He stresses that the public has always visited Castle Howard. Paterson's *Annual Survey of 1829* reads: "The liberality of the noble proprietor, in admitting the public to view this elegant repository, entitles him to grateful applause." Mr. Howard proudly maintains this tradition, in the belief that it keeps the very house happy to continue the pattern it has always known. He feels that when a room is not truly lived in, it becomes lifeless—perhaps a fascinating museum, but still dead. And Castle Howard, in each of its rooms, assuredly lives.

PRECEDING PAGE: *A vast greensward heralds the Baroque grandeur of Castle Howard, designed in 1699 by Sir John Vanbrugh for Charles Howard, 3rd earl of Carlisle, and completed some fifty years later.* ABOVE: *In the Great Hall, Pellegrini paintings adorn the walls and chimneypiece. Classical Roman sculptures were collected in the 18th century by the 4th earl of Carlisle. In the foreground a dummy board figure, of a type popular in the 17th and 18th centuries, sweeps imaginary dust.* RIGHT: *A wrought-iron balustrade made by John Gardom around 1710 rims a balcony beneath the luminous cupola.* FOLLOWING PAGES: *Gilded Charles II tables echo the symmetry of stone pilasters carved in 1705. A niche made of scagliola gives emphasis to the balanced setting.*

RIGHT: *An imposing plaster cast of Michelangelo's Lorenzo de' Medici ennobles a gracefully curving balcony. At left, an early-19th-century circular convex mirror reflects the stately setting.*

OPPOSITE: *John Linnell, an important 18th-century English cabinetmaker, carver and designer, made all the furnishings—including the canopy bed—specifically for this Bedroom, around 1780. The simplified elegance of his designs finds an appropriate graphic complement in a series of prints of Raphael's designs for the Vatican loggia. The English silk brocade bedcovering echoes the dominant tones of the room, while a Feraghan rug injects warm color. Mirrors, facing one another, create an infinity of reflections.*

151

CREDITS

WRITERS

The following writers prepared the original *Architectural Digest* articles from which the material in this book has been adapted:

Susan Heller Anderson
Helen Barnes
Peter Carlsen
Adrian Cook
Bruno de Hamel
Elizabeth Dickson
Jean-Louis Gaillemin
Alexandra Henderson
Richard Horn
Gavin Stamp
Sir Humphry Wakefield

All original text adapted by Cameron Curtis McKinley.

All original captions adapted by Kirsten Grimstad.

PHOTOGRAPHERS

Robert Emmett Bright 24–31, 90–99, 116–123, 124–129, 136–143
Bruno de Hamel 130–135
Oberto Gili 100–107
Pascal Hinous 10–15, 32–37, 38–45, 54–61, 62–71, 72–77, 78–83
Derry Moore 2–9, 16–23, 46–53, 84–89, 108–115, 144–151

DESIGN

Design Direction:
Philip Kaplan, Executive Graphics Director
Knapp Communications Corporation

Book Design and Production:
Glen Iwasaki
Felice Mataré